IT'S TIME TO LEARN CATTLE

It's Time to Learn Cattle

Walter the Educator

Silent King Books
A WhichHead Entertainment Imprint

Copyright © 2025 by Walter the Educator

All rights reserved. No part of this book may be reproduced in any manner whatsoever without written per- mission except in the case of brief quotations embodied in critical articles and reviews.

First Printing, 2024

Disclaimer

This book is a literary work; the story is not about specific persons, locations, situations, and/or circumstances unless mentioned in a historical context. Any resemblance to real persons, locations, situations, and/or circumstances is coincidental. This book is for entertainment and informational purposes only. The author and publisher offer this information without warranties expressed or implied. No matter the grounds, neither the author nor the publisher will be accountable for any losses, injuries, or other damages caused by the reader's use of this book. The use of this book acknowledges an understanding and acceptance of this disclaimer.

It's Time to Learn Cattle is a collectible early learning book by Walter the Educator suitable for all ages belonging to Walter the Educator's Time to Eat Book Series. Collect more books at WaltertheEducator.com

USE THE EXTRA SPACE TO TAKE NOTES AND DOCUMENT YOUR MEMORIES

CATTLE

Out in the fields so big and wide,

It's Time to Learn about

Cattle

Cattle graze side by side.

With strong, stout legs and tails so long,

They moo and munch all day long.

Some have spots and some are plain,

Some like sunshine, some like rain.

Brown or black or white as snow,

Each one's special, this we know!

Cattle eat the grass so green,

Chewing slow, it keeps them keen.

They have four parts inside their belly,

Turning grass to milk so mellow!

A baby cow is called a calf,

It stumbles first, then walks with class.

It drinks its milk and grows up strong,

Running, jumping all day long!

It's Time to Learn about

Cattle

Boy cows, girl cows, do you know?

A bull will lead, the cows will follow.

A group of cattle is called a herd,

They stick together, just like birds!

Some have horns, and some have none,

But all love standing in the sun.

They flick their tails to shoo the flies,

And swish them off from legs and eyes.

Farmers care for cattle well,

Giving food and clean warm stalls.

Cows give milk for cheese and butter,

And work in fields when tractors falter.

They talk with moos, they stomp around,

Their hooves make such a heavy sound!

They love a pond to take a sip,

It's Time to Learn about

Cattle

Then swish their tails and give a flip!

Cattle help in many ways,

On farms, they work through all the days.

They give us milk and help grow grain,

Through sunshine bright and pouring rain.

So next time when you hear a moo,

Remember cattle help us too!

Strong and gentle, big and bright,

It's Time to Learn about

Cattle

Cattle make the world just right!

ABOUT THE CREATOR

Walter the Educator is one of the pseudonyms for Walter Anderson. Formally educated in Chemistry, Business, and Education, he is an educator, an author, a diverse entrepreneur, and he is the son of a disabled war veteran. "Walter the Educator" shares his time between educating and creating. He holds interests and owns several creative projects that entertain, enlighten, enhance, and educate, hoping to inspire and motivate you. Follow, find new works, and stay up to date with Walter the Educator™

at WaltertheEducator.com

www.ingramcontent.com/pod-product-compliance
Lightning Source LLC
LaVergne TN
LVHW051920060526
838201LV00060B/4086